How to Know
ThySelf

A detailed handbook to the journey ahead of self-discovery

Shurunda K Harris

Table of Contents

Introduction..1

Know Thyself...3

The Importance Of Knowing Thyself...8

Know Thy Power...10

Know Thy Strength..13

Acknowledge And Explain Your Ambition......................................14

Stand Up For You And Others..16

Evaluate Your Opinions...17

Build A Support Network 19

Why Not Talking About Your Flaws Makes You Weak.....................21

Conclusion 24

Introduction

L ife is a series of processes. We are all aware that there is no quick process except to go by the stages. With confusion comes clarity, but before then, a process has to occur. You might often be tired of the status quo and need a change despite being unsure of the next path. But you're confident in you despite what may. You are sure a process needs to occur that will open your eyes to certain realities.

The defined name is not far-fetched; but termed a journey to self-discovery: A journey you need to take to be fulfilled and discover your purpose in life. Many have experienced it; many are yet to, while many are close. Everyone has to pass through this process at a point in time in their life.

Discovery is one of the necessities of life and existence. I'm sure you don't want to live your life anyhow. Trust me; you'll want to make an impact and fulfill destiny in life. Isn't that more reasons to self-discovery? Living anyhow could bring darkness, emptiness, and lack of focus, unhappiness, anger, and resentment. Many people have died unfulfilled with talents and potentials... It is a blessing to have discovered and experienced "knowing yourself", however, there are similar grounds to a wide range of experiences, some are positive, while others may be negative. There are the usual potholes in every stage of life, is it the confusion, tiredness, and constant lack of motivation? What is it that gives us that spark to begin a self-discovery journey? It is a good move, and it shouldn't just end at that. This uncovering of light that chases your darkness away, is when you begin to function much more effectively, you have great, intense joy and fulfillment more than ever before--nothing as satisfying as discovering yourself. As we all know, the journey in an unknown place can be stressful and tiring without guidance, there is a lot of work at every destination that needs to be accomplished, and this is what this book will do, it can be used as a guide.

Know Thyself

To know thyself, what does it imply? It is a ancient Greek aphorism, but what exactly does it mean? Checking the lists of persons and possible word creators whom this can be attributed to, the list is slightly higher than ten. Socrates is perhaps the most common speaker of the phrase "know yourself." Some of the other possible creators are Pythagoras, Bias Priene, Myson de Chenae, no matter who made the phrase, what does it mean? "Know thyself" is the proclamation that appeared in the front of the temple in Delphi. yet, it's meaning and significance is, I know not.

First and foremost, it means to understand your attitude, it is crucial because it enables you to be conscious of your limitations, however you can only improve from a positive perspective or make better life decisions only when you know that attitude.

Gone are the centuries when the unconscious's discovery originates from a critical addition to that Delphic injunction. As such, it looks like all that is known is our deep-seated feelings, desires, beliefs, and intentions that we can better ourselves.

Thus, if you start progressing the issue from the Delphic injunction, there seems to be a certain distance between each subject and themselves. One's character is not only what we manifest in acting and living as we do, it can also be an object for each of us to study and make sense of. Some forces and limitations make you act as you do, it consists of one's dispositional mental states; let it be conscious or unconscious, which can be the objects in "The Varieties of Self-Knowledge," which I call "third personal self-knowledge." That is to say, to understand those mental states; you need to interact with a relatively complex epistemic method that has no guarantee of being successful, they are broadly akin to the ones we use to gain knowledge of other people's minds, yet, when successfully executed, these procedures give you a clear picture of yourself, although it can be hard to comprehend and challenging to attain, it can be valuable because it reveals the important truths to us about ourselves, based on which we can eventually make decisions that can improve the quality of our lives.

A significant difference exists between the application of these epistemic procedures in one's case and that of other people. Frequently, in our case and our case only, the prompts we have to start with are our inner feelings and other concurrent mental states. We are aware of these mental states in a "first-personal" way. The supreme guarantee of "The Varieties of Self-Knowledge" is that a complete self-information record should be a record of both first-and-third-individual self-information. Strangely, the contemporary discussion on self-information, in general would be unaware of this somewhat clear objective. From one viewpoint, behaviorists for example, have attempted to decrease all of the self-knowledge to third-personal self- knowledge. In a similar vein, contemporary scientists informed philosophers like Peter Carruthers and Eric Schwitzgebel have tried to deny the existence of first- personal self-knowledge. They draw on recent empirical data, which shows how ignorant or mistaken we can be regarding our minds. Contemporary proponents' of an inferential conception of self-knowledge, like Quassim Cassam, have tried to diminish the role of first-personal self- knowledge by arguing that, at most, it would give us knowledge of somewhat irrelevant mental states – like presently feeling pain in one's foot right. By contrast, in his view, essential truths about oneself could only be revealed through deduction of the best clarification beginning with the perception of one's behavior and inner promptings. While I agree that the latter kind of knowledge is undoubtedly more interesting, it should be recognized that it would only be impossible without the knowledge of one's concurrent mental states.

Furthermore, while positively and not revelatory of one's character, one's first-personal knowledge of one's bodily sensations like pain, for instance, clearly serves as an invaluable role. What makes it like that is to enable us to dodge specific threats.

A great measure of consideration is committed to first-individual self-information with next to no work done on third-individual self-information. Why? Because of what I would call a sort of philosophical snobbery. Allow me to clarify that. Descartes philosophers were astounded by the trademark characteristics of first-individual self-information. Our brains appear to be "straightforward" to us, despite what is happening inside them, it suddenly becomes apparent to us. The excruciating or pleasurable sensations I am feeling right now are "self-implying." If I feel pain in my foot, I am quickly mindful of it. If I have pertinent ideas, I can immediately self-attribute that sensation, unless there are motivations to question my truthfulness—we ward off the impression of being "definitive" regarding our psychological states.

However, such knowledge is not independent of experience, and neither is it based on an observation of our mental states. Through the observation of our behavior and inference to its likely cause, we seem to be confronted with a severe epistemological issue, how does that information occur? How might it display those attributes which appear to separate it from all sorts of exact information? The trouble of comprehending this epistemological issue has driven numerous philosophers to dispose of the third-individual self-information as philosophically uninteresting, because in all case they have eventually thought of it as just one more example of information dependent on surmising to the best clarification.

Indeed some contemporary theorists, like Richard Moran, have gone so far as to argue that when we deliberate what to believe, desire, and intend, based on weighing reasons, we are capable of first-personal self-knowledge. While in all other cases—that is to say, in those instances where knowledge about ourselves are obtained through third-personal means and, interestingly, also when we make self-ascriptions of concurrent sensations—we would not be operating in that mode. There wouldn't be anything epistemologically distinctive.

I concur that there is something epistemologically confusing about first-individual self- information and that needs some sort of philosophical clarification. However, third-individual self-information, as well, is epistemologically fascinating when one understands the assortment of strategies. While I agree that there is something distinctive about our knowledge of what I would call our "commissive propositional attitudes." I do think that self-ascriptions of sensations are also a manifestation of first-personal self-knowledge. Even though, we will see they do call for a subtly different account than the one we might want to give for our knowledge of our propositional attitudes.

I believe that historians often interpret "self- interpreting" as "knowing your place in the scheme of things - where you fit into society." Maybe the original intention was to remind people of their limits, the dual approach recommended by Annalisa Coliva, allowing both individuals' and third parties, sounds resonant to me. Despite all external evidence from a "third party," we can often know what is happening to us through a small but persistent and completely closed private insight.

On the other hand, the whole world of personal insights can collapse and, with a word or two from a friend or person who is well familiar with us, this also brings a question to my mind "can we really have knowledge of someone else?" This would be the same as third party knowledge (which seems to be a matter of method and data available) but is different from what is known to the connoisseur. "You" is different from "she" and "him." These can be things, such as a compliment or a conflict that you don't have in third party reports.

One philosophical stance that interests us a lot is someone else's knowledge of ourselves. It is not the same as what we know about ourselves in the first-person or from a third-person perspective. Rather than discussing this, I feel that we can learn a lot about ourselves and others by examining the other person's approach to ourselves, still from third parties' perspective. If you'd instead call it self-knowledge based on someone else's self-knowledge testimony, there is no problem. In either case, the critical fact is that the testimony is a source of self-knowledge. The stimuli for the brain reveal mental states that can be recognized as two parts:

1. A state of mind (associated with a brain disease) in a person's feelings, emotions, and tendencies. Everything is based on neural reactions. These are first-person and functions

2. Mental activity (linked to brain activity) is linked to neural stimuli and reactions.

The mental parts that correlate with neural responses are the current self-interaction. We can call them mental responses to stimuli. We can directly see the state of mind at a higher level of consciousness. The lower level consciousness can perceive part of the activity. Our character can be indirectly recognized through various behavioral observations. These are the characteristics of the third personality which is not about brain activity.

The Importance of
Knowing ThySelf

A lot comes from knowing thyself. Nobody can know you better than you. No wonder variations exist among us, which makes us all unique in our ways and capabilities. As stated earlier, increased self-knowledge has a wide-range of positive ramifications. What you know can never be taken from you. However, expanded passionate insight is one of the most significant positive impacts. This is where you realize that you are best at what you're passionate about, no matter how difficult it looks. It is at this juncture that you distinguish ability from passion. At the point when you discovered that you're the most emotionally intelligent, you had better be ready to recognize and deal with your emotions, neither curbing them nor being lost in them. Learn to control it rather than it controlling you.

Emotionally smart people are also more at peace with themselves and focus more on meeting their standards rather than others' standards. Self-knowledge and high intelligence are also correlated with greater levels of success. For example, recent psychological studies indicate that many top business leader's have these two traits, which play a crucial role in their continued achievements.

So, whether you want to excel in your job, looking for improvements in the most critical relationships in your life, or want to experience more peace within you, you have a lot to gain from working on Knowing thyself. All these realizations and achievements are only possible when you know thyself.

Know Thy Power

The truth is that you can give meaning to a sentence depending on the interpretation you give or what you think it means to you. It is an applied saying and can easily be translated if you know your limits, your motivations, or know yourself. The original proverb may not speak ill of those who decide their fate (according to Prometheus Bound by Aeschylus, which may be their first use in literature). But when we know ourselves, we can use it as a word of caution and motivation. We, in turn, understand our capabilities.

In the modern world, we want to be familiar with each other, and with the tools at our disposal, we all believe in the truth that we know ourselves better than anyone else. It can be true, and it is. However, the fog of what we do not know about ourselves has never been considered in what to apply and how it thus benefit us most. Knowing yourself means how much introspection applies to our personality in terms of testifying to our strengths and weaknesses.

The world is dynamic, and in a sentence that is applicable in an entirely different world, it is revealed that introspection will remain essential, just as it was. For instance, a time when you wanted to do something beyond your limits and failed to remember that you're still in the learning process. Whatever happens, there is no penalty for what you are yet to experience.

But if that is your motive, it means that you know yourself well enough and see the benefits of your experience. Our courage is continuously being tested, and our motivation keeps fighting.

Knowing how we act and how we overcome obstacles means we know ourselves and that we are growing in areas where we cannot and will not succeed immediately. Let me discuss another point, which is whether we can be as introspective as we seem. Do you know yourself? In some cases, it could be termed as a silly question as we obviously think we know ourselves, but it's a question of deep thought that needs a sincere answer. Truth be told, you can't lie to yourself, we have been with these personalities all our lives and have had time to learn about ourselves and our actions.

 We know what drives us, what we ignore, and why? There's a reason psychology and philosophy are still relevant topics, this is because we all have the same barrier to our unconscious interpretation of ourselves and how others see us, it's something we can never really understand if we are not willing to open our mind, although we can imagine how it might be, we can never do it to the extent that we can learn our outer perspective. What is the limit to knowing yourself? We may never know. However, this is one of the elements of self-examination. What we believe about ourselves may not even be true, but the achievement of this knowledge is sufficient to gain insight into self-action.

It is something that we can never achieve as a whole as we want, however, that will not prevent us from wanting to know something about ourselves and how it is applicable today. Know your successes and failures. To use the phrase "do you know yourself in modern times," we must allow ourselves to see the questions that the Greek philosophers and writers had in formulating this phrase. "How perfect do you do what you do"? Do we know the limits of our strength? Do we have to behave successfully to be successful? Although they may seem like irrelevant questions, finding an answer leads to answers. This can be achieved when you conduct a thorough research on yourself.

Insight is the primary goal, and whether that insight is far or near perfection, introspection is irrelevant to everyday life in this day and age. Know yourself and learn to understand your motivation and work ethic. Experience all you want to experience, assess the situations you find yourself in and determine how your personality application plays a specific role that you have unconsciously chosen. Self-observation is an engaging and exhilarating experience as the answers can never be corroborated, but can only be applicable as answers when we see their benefits.

Philosophy will always have a stand in the world, as it is based on everything that happens now and forever. The questions of life are about how much questions are we willing to ask. The modern application I see in it takes time for self-examination to take advantage of those willing to look for additional enhancements searching for answers.

Your power lies in all of the above mentioned and, more importantly, in insight, introspection, and knowledge. When you know thy power, it is of no use until you put it into action. This is because action speaks better than words. Utilizing thy power sent to you from the universe is one big step to knowing yourself.

Know Thy Strength

You might not be sure of your capabilities when you don't know your strength. There is more to what you can achieve or accomplish when there's a need. It is simply best to Know Thy strength! It is not as simple as A, B, C. But as the saying "you die in the ignorance of what you don't know." You might not be able to utilize your strengths when you haven't identified/recognized it. Because it's almost impossible to recognize every individual's strengths, it will be best for you if you know they strength. It will help you in all phases of your life. I would concentrate on how you could build your strength by following these few steps to own your strength.

Acknowledge and Explain your Ambition

More often than not, humans have a negative opinion about ambition. We all can't be the same in life. You must know and build around what you like, know, and best at. Nothing good comes easy, and for you to succeed, you have to sacrifice. Many want to succeed, but they feel uncomfortable when they admit it and show others that they are committed to their careers. You owe no one an apology for being ambitious. Never apologize for the purpose! We all know what we want out of life, and the decision is yours to make. Inform others you know about your career goals and look for mentors and sponsors to help you achieve your goal, being held accountable will help enable you to attain your goals, it will motivate you not to quit until you achieve your goal. When you hesitate to voice your ambitions, it keeps you small and depletes your strength. There is great power in word of mouth, and once you can think/dream it, you can achieve it replace negative self-talk with positive affirmations. Nothing can sabotage you more than negative self-talk dominating your thoughts. Negative self-talk paralyzes you from taking action, prevents you from progressing, taking risks and exploring new opportunities. Learn always to be positive. Negative thoughts will drain your fuel tank, and if you run out of fuel; you will run out of strength. Listen to these negative voices, mark them as such, and never allow them to pull you down. Confidence is the first step to possessing your strength. Believe in yourself, even when no one else does.

Don't let these boundaries control your life and success. Let go of your negative thoughts, always change them, and replace them with positive thoughts. Remember that no one can bring you down except you. This is possible when you give room for those negative things in your life.

Stand Up for You and Others

There is a saying that you cannot give what you don't have. Before you can fight for others, you need to have successfully have fought severally for yourself. Once you understand your worth and how you contribute to successful results, you can position yourself as someone who can help others achieve their goals. You can help others in diverse ways. Take for instance; you can help a company achieve its goals by communicating regularly with your manager about how your work is producing positive results. You achieve this by looking for projects where you can add value to create visibility and credibility. It is powerful! Also, your colleagues should not be left out. Try to strengthen and defend them where necessary. Show respect and pride for your work, and others around you, and they will respond in the same way. Treat everyone the way you would like them to treat you. Promoting your team and achievements makes you a great leader. You don't need to be proud and claim to know all, ask for help when you need it, when you don't ask, you might not know who is willing to help. Asking for help when needed, doesn't belittle you. Somehow we believe that when we admit that we don't have all the answers it's deemed in a negative way, many influential people know when to seek help and feedback from others. Asking about and assessing the resources required to succeed will increase your chances of success. It takes confidence to seek help. What you don't know, you don't know. Therefore, asking for help is a of strength.

Evaluate your Opinions

I'm sure there have been times when someone came up with the same idea that you had in mind which came out to be a great idea, but because you were not sure about what people would think, or say about your idea, you decided to keep quiet. Why didn't you voice that idea? Sure, you want people to think you are great, and you might fear your idea would not be received well but does that matter? Each of your ideas might not be welcomed, but there are likely a few. You have your power when you share your thought process and intelligence with others. Do you even know that the more opinion you share, the more boldness you have next time? People will ask for your opinion at some point. It is necessary! Acknowledge your fears as well as your negative thoughts, because it sabotages your success, and takes away your strength. Be confident in yourself and know that there is room for improvement, although we all doubt, we lose our power if we allow our fears to dominate us and paralyze us into not taking action. Own your power by facing your fears. Conquer it at all costs. Understand that when you surrender to controls and powers, you let your fears dominate your life.

You might be thinking; how can I be free? Start little- Step by step, leave your comfort zone and build muscles of self-confidence. Every new risk you take and every new step brings you closer to holding your power. Reflect on yourself and schedule a moment of silence. In a work-rewarding culture, it is a challenge not to feel guilty when you are planning a time when to be disconnected and simply "with" yourself. However, at this time, creativity is born. It is powerful! You will be amazed at how a moment of silence in the day helps you find solutions to old problems and enhances your career through strategic lenses.

Therefore, reconnecting with yourself non-stop can help you find your passion and purpose, which leads to personal power. Use your strength to incorporate moments of silence into your daily routine.

Build a Support Network

You cannot create a successful career in a vacuum. The atmosphere and associations you find yourself have a significant impact on your success. Get advice from mentors and sponsors, and ensure you effectively utilize it. Look for strong models who are successful in their careers, whom you can mirror by watching them display their various processes and achievements. Create mutual relationships with people of like minds or similar goals who can help you and will support your ideas and give you the knowledge to be successful the kind of people who won't allow you to rest on your oasis. When you think about growth, know that your network matters a lot. It would be best to have those that will always motivate, push, and ensure you're producing results.

Knowledge is power, and whoever has a cycle of mental growth is open to learning. Be curious. Be open, listen, and learn from others. Every day offers a new opportunity for personal gain. No knowledge is a waste and you don't learn by remaining dormant. You may not be an expert at all, but your enthusiasm to learn leads to personal growth and personal power—practice self-care when you have an opinion on growth. It has taken me a while to learn how powerful and essential self-care is, I believed in the mantra that the more you work, the more successful you will be. Just like saying more work, more money because nothing good comes easy. Hence, the need to continue working hard but that should not be to the detriment of your health. Hard work is essential, but you lose steam, and energy if you don't spend time refueling. This renewed energy comes from taking care of yourself. Only you know how to fill your body and soul better, therefore, it is advisable to opt in for what best can refuel your energy, for some, it's excercise or meditating, for others it's taking a trip, whatever you choose, make it priority. It will help maintain your power over a more extended period.

Why Not Talking About Your Flaws Makes You Weak

No one is perfect, and the fact that we fail to recognize our flaws makes us have little faith that we can strengthen our weaknesses. From time to time, I interact with people who cannot be honest about their fears or mistakes. I believe there is a reason why people act like that, and that really bothers me. We prefer to talk and boast about our strengths and forget the talks on our weaknesses. If you show me your strengths all the time at some point, my intelligence will tell me that you are not being honest with me. Do not get me wrong. I'm not looking for someone to take the stage or social media and list their shortcomings one after the other that is not what I am looking for, confessing confidential information without public consideration is self-defeating. I understand that we need to reserve specific details of our lives for individual relationships. However, when I can't sit down with you and have occasional moments of mutual vulnerability, I lose interest in the relationship.

The adage "is too good to be true" applies to more than classic ad schemes and pyramids, these also apply to people. To gain my respect, you have to be honest and it starts with being honest to yourself. To protect ourselves, we treat the world as a card game, and approach with a poker face and extreme distrust of other people's motives. I understand, I did. It's difficult to tell other people about our mistakes, we are afraid that they will take advantage of it or control us, but in the end we are unknown and unloved. If I don't know your weakness, how can I be of help? Because you've refused to open up, you feel left alone all by yourself. Relentless self-protection comes at a high price. Would you like to know how other people perceive people trying to appear strong when they are weak? If we point out one of their mistakes, they attack us. When asked about their weaknesses, they play or use vague language to avoid ownership. These are not signs of strength. They are a repulsion tactic, and it can be obvious. You do not need to glorify in your strength but rather in your weakness because only in your weakness can you be strengthened.

Your lack of weakness makes you weak, if you want a person to see you as strong, you have to face your weaknesses. It would help if you were trustworthy and sincere with some people about your fears, struggles, sin, and pain. You don't need to reveal all these to everyone. Since there are people you trust who won't use that against you, you are good to confess to them, a problem shared is usually half solved, as soon as you try to do this the lesser the problem becomes.

Here's one thing: I don't need anyone to be my strength; you don't need anyone to be your strength that power is within you. You don't need to get everything right, you don't always have to be strong, but you have to be honest.

Nobody can strengthen you, yes, you can be promoted, selected, and even adored, and when you take on influential roles, people assume you have the power, but that assumption will fade in time unless you have your strength because authentic power doesn't come from an outside source or a critical title, real personal power is generated from within and backed up within.

When you have your power, you gain credibility to be successful. You will find colleagues and critical stakeholders, influential and persuasive people seeking your opinion and help. Possessing your power increases self-confidence and an understanding of how you can help others make decisions and achieve their goals. With power, you can build and maintain strong relationships at work and outside. It enables you to defend yourself, negotiate for yourself, show strength, and admit when you are wrong. It takes strength to be vulnerable and compassionate without getting lost in the process. The positive news is that we all have potentials. The hint is to connect with it and own it.

Conclusion

I have hopefully brought you some useful tools that could be used on your journey of self-discovery. It is an essential knowledge you should embrace. This is not just a self-development guide; its practical and usefull. It has in it proven research of knowledge and truth that work. It is garnered off my own experiences and what has worked for others. However, it's not magic, so you will have to work to initiate goals that will bring results.